A GAME of THRONES

PUZZLE BOOK

THIS IS A CARLTON BOOK

This edition first published in 2016 by Carlton Books Ltd
An imprint of the Carlton Publishing Group
20 Mortimer Street
London W1T 3JW

A CIP catalogue for this book is available from the British Library.

Illustrations were supplied by the following sources: *120 Great Paintings
from Medieval Illustrated Books*, edited by Carol Belanger Grafton;
Costume and Ornament of the Middle Ages in Full Color by Henry
Shaw; *Full Color Heraldic Designs* (Dover Books); *Full Color Medieval
Ornament* (Dover Books); *Medieval Knights, Armor & Weapons* (Dover
Books); *Renaissance & Medieval Costume* by Camille Bonnard; *Treasury
of Medieval Illustrations* by Paul Lacroix

ISBN 978-1-78097-784-3

Printed in Dubai

10 9 8 7 6 5 4 3 2 1

A GAME of THRONES PUZZLE BOOK

PUZZLES AND QUIZZES INSPIRED BY THE TV SERIES AND FANTASY NOVELS

- UNOFFICIAL AND UNAUTHORIZED -

TIM DEDOPULOS

CARLTON
BOOKS

CONTENTS

THE QUEST

CONTENTS

THE BIG ADVENTURE

	Q	A

INTRODUCTION

George R. R. Martin began writing his masterwork political fantasy series *A Song of Ice and Fire* in 1991. Although the first novel, *A Game of Thrones*, was published to little acclaim in 1996, the series has gone on to take the world by storm. More than 24 million copies have been sold in America alone. The books draw much of their inspiration from medieval European history, including the British Wars of the Roses. The HBO television series based on the books, *Game of Thrones*, has likewise proved itself a world-beater.

One of the toughest parts of writing a puzzle book like this is balancing the needs of the problems with the sanctity of a much-loved setting. I've done my best to present an entertaining range of mental challenges without trampling all over GRRM's fabulous lore. The puzzles in this volume are set across the entire time range of the books, and I've done my best to ensure that nothing in here specifically contradicts *A Song of Ice and Fire*'s canon.

I've also tried to make sure that I don't have individuals behaving too badly out of character, or involved in things that would seem implausible. You're more likely to find that questions of tangled kinship involve Walder Frey's brood than Daenerys Targaryen, for example. Where feasible, I've ascribed specialities to characters who remained somewhat uncertain – the teaching of mathematics, for example, I assigned to Archmaester Mollos, rather than Archmaester Walgrave – and placed invented characters in Houses that to date have been mentioned only in passing.

But don't worry about needing to have the novels memorized. Of all the puzzles in here, only the ten quizzes require a knowledge of the series. Everything else is readily solvable with a bit of logic, deduction and patience. Gauging the difficulty of puzzles is a tricky business – different minds find different things tough – but in general, each season's questions will be a little harder than those of the one before.

The most important thing, of course, is to have fun. Puzzle-solving is, like story-telling, one of the few recreational habits found in all human societies, from the most ancient right up to the present day. So put on your thinking head and dive in. Westeros (and beyond) awaits you!

Tim Dedopulos, London

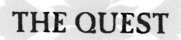

THE QUEST

KIRRA'S APPLES

The peace of Cider Hall was ruffled when Kirra came stamping up to Ser Bryan, bristling with anger. "Ser Fossoway, that ape Tregard is out of order. I beg you, please speak to him."

Ser Bryan sighed. "What is it this time, woman?"

"I need to know how this week's apple-picking has been. How am I supposed to do my job otherwise? All he'll tell me is that if I take the number of barrels gathered, and then add to that a quarter of that number, I'd come to 15 barrels. What's wrong with the man?"

"He likes you."

How many barrels of apples are there?

Solution on page 106

SQUARED SERS

Ser Manfryd Yew and Ser Raynard Ruttiger fell to conversation during a feast at Casterly Rock. To their astonishment, they discovered that they had more in common than just their liege lord.

Each had a wife, a son and a daughter. When added together, the ages of the Yews totalled 100 years – as did that of the Ruttigers. Furthermore, if each family member's age was squared, then the squared ages of wife, son and daughter added together equalled the father's squared age in both cases. The only difference was that Ser Manfryd's daughter was one year younger than her brother, while Ser Raynard's daughter was two years younger.

How old are the two knights and their families?

Solution on page 106

FOWLER PLAY

Jeyne and Jennelyn Fowler were identical –
slender and pretty, with wispy yellow hair.
Prince Quentyn could never tell them apart, and
today, they'd ensured that their outfits matched
perfectly. As he approached, they favoured him
with devilish smiles.

"Good day, Prince…"

"…Quentyn. We hope…"

"…you are well."

Quentyn bowed nervously. "Ladies."

"Oh no, that…"

"…won't do…"

"…at all. Surely…"

"…you know us?"

"I am Jeyne, am I not?" said the one on the left.

"I am Jennelyn, am I not?" said the one on the right.

Before Quentyn could reply, Ferne, their lady in waiting, leaned forward to whisper in his ear. "One of them is lying, my lord. I swear this to be true."

Which is which?

Solution on page 107

OLD WYK

During the years of preparation before being given to the sea a second time, acolytes of th Drowned God must train, learn and be purified. Their keep stands on the shores of Nagga's Cradle, a tall, grey building as stern as the sea itself.

New acolytes were housed in a square block broken into a three-by-three grid of cells, three acolytes to a cell. The central cell held the master of the dormitory Cerron, an old, blind Drowned Man. The years weighed heavily on him but he retained wits enough remember that so long as each side of the dormitory held nine acolytes, all was well.

It did not take the 24 acolytes long to realize that Cerron could be fooled. It proved simple to arrange themselves so that a full quarter of their number cou slip away from the dormitory to drink and gossip on the shores of the bay.

How did they do it?

Solution on page 107

19

THE MAESTER'S HAND

"**Y**ou, boy. Roone. Hold your right palm in front of your mouth and blow slowly onto it.

"Maester?"

"Just do it, boy. There. How does it feel?"

"Damp, Maester, and warm."

"Quite right. Now, replace your right palm with your left, purse your lips, and blow on it strongly. Come on, quickly. How does that feel?"

"Cool, Maester."

"Just so. Why?"

Solution on page 108

DRAGONSTONE

On the island of Dragonstone, hidden deep below the dungeons of the Stone Drum, an ancient Targayen tomb was carved into the living obsidian of Dragonmont. Within it lie two husbands with their two wives, two fathers with their two daughters, two grandmothers with their two granddaughters, two mothers with their two sons, two sisters with their two brothers, and two girls with their two mothers. Just six names are given, one for each inhabitant.

How is this possible?

Solution on page 108

LORD DAERON VAITH

L ord Daeron Vaith of the Red Dunes glared at the three men in front of him. The dock workers had been squabbling for some days now, and it had escalated to the point where the feud was becoming problematic. He was tempted to punish all three, but capriciousness was a last resort.

Stripped down to their barest bones and freed of the assorted accusations and counter claims, the arguments of the three men could be summarized as follows:

Gage: Alarn is lying.

Alarn: Rafe is lying.

Rafe: Both Gage and Alarn are lying.

Which man is telling the truth?

Solution on page 108

A QUIZ OF ICE AND FIRE I

1. Who helps Robb Stark save his brother Bran from wildlings?

2. What was the name of Tyrion Lannister's first wife?

3. Which exiled knight enters service with Viserys and Daenerys Targaryen in Essos?

4. How did Davos Seaworth save Storm's End from starvation?

5. Which character in the Game of Thrones TV show does Emilia Clarke play?

6. What is the name of the ancestral castle of House Tully?

7. Who is Sansa Stark married to?

8. Who exposes Arya Stark's identity to the Brotherhood Without Banners?

9. To whom do House Swyft owe allegiance?

10. What is the name of the assassin who agrees to kill three victims for Arya Stark?

Solution on page 109

VARYS

M y clothing's fine as velvet rare,

Though under earth my dwellings lie,

And when above it I appear,

My enemies do me decry.

The gardener's hate
for me is fine,

I spoil his works as
he does mine.

Who am I?

Solution on page 110

FAIRMARKET

Built at the blue fork of the river Trident, Fairmarket is known throughout the Riverlands as a fine place for trading grain. Lumm, a trader by need more than by inclination, has a hundred bushels of high-quality barley, just eight percent chaff. To make it go further, his plan is to swap it for a larger quantity of cheaper barley, a third chaff, to then sell on in the city to those who don't know much better.

How many bushels of the cheaper barley would provide a fair exchange?

Solution on page 110

HOUSE MARTELL

In the Water Gardens of Sunspear, four lesser knights of House Martell were sitting discussing events. After a time, talk turned to family and the nature of their various interrelationships.

Harlen turned to Selmont and said, "Petyr has the same relationship to Theodor as I do to you, you know."

Selmont nodded. "Yes. After all, you are to Theodor as Petyr is to you."

How are the men related?

Solution on page 111

THE BAY OF CRABS

Daffyn and Whelan fell to arguing over who was faster on foot, and once coin was laid on the outcome, a proper race became inevitable. Jhon Mooton agreed to referee, picked a course along the shore of the Bay of Crabs a mile-and-a-half in length, and stationed people at the quarter-marks and at halfway.

When all was said and done, Daffyn won but by less than a full stride, and the two were neck-and-neck all the way. To general amazement, the first half of the race took exactly the same amount of time as the second half. The men hit the three-quarter point in six-and-three-quarters minutes, and it took as long from halfway to three-quarters as it did from the three-quarter mark to the end.

How long did the race take?

Solution on page 111

FIRST IMPRESSIONS

D o you have the wit to see,

Ragged though our mien might be,

A hint of glitter in our veins?

Grind off dust and gold remains.

Often sought by men are we,

None who know us can disagree.

So tell me then – who are we?

Solution on page 111

A HUNT FOR WORDS 1

```
R  N  N  W  O  T  S  Y  A  W  O  R  R  A  H
H  E  A  R  T  E  A  T  E  R  V  Y  J  M  R
W  V  L  N  S  H  E  L  B  Q  L  G  N  B  H
E  E  A  W  O  J  G  Y  L  I  M  Y  Y  E  L
D  S  S  W  O  E  X  R  Q  A  O  G  T  R  L
Y  E  E  K  R  F  T  N  E  O  R  E  L  L  O
T  H  R  G  S  W  I  J  D  E  L  I  N  Y  R
K  T  E  N  N  J  R  P  S  Y  N  E  A  V  Q
C  N  S  H  I  E  L  D  K  M  L  A  N  S  A
A  R  E  Y  F  N  Y  M  E  R  I  A  W  N  M
L  O  D  A  F  Y  K  H  A  D  O  K  H  A  A
B  B  J  F  I  A  J  F  O  R  A  X  M  K  Y
N  E  F  E  R  J  Y  H  T  N  I  L  F  E  I
G  R  I  G  G  Q  N  U  G  V  U  Y  Q  S  X
S  T  K  G  S  A  R  G  O  N  I  V  A  C  M
```

AENYS	HARROWAYS TOWN	OLENNA
AMBERLY	HEARTEATER	ORELL
BLACKTYDE	JAFER	QAMAYI
FARLEN	JAYNE	RHLLOR
FLINT	JINQI	ROBERT
FOWLER	KHADOKH	SARGON
GERGEN	KHEWO	SHIELD
GREENAWAY	MARIYA	SNAKES
GRIFFINS ROOST	NEFER	TALLA
GRIGG	NYMERIA	THE SEVEN

Solution on page 112

DORNISH TROUBLE

Lord Varner had urgent business with House Qorgyle, in the Dornish deserts, so he sent his man Abelarn to castle Sandstone to open discussions. The road past the Hellholt is long and murderously hot at times and Abelarn found the journey increasingly difficult.

Four days out from Sandstone, he knew that he needed to find a specific place of shelter that night. If he travelled at 10 miles per hour, he'd pass the shelter a full hour after sunset and risk missing it altogether. If he travelled at 15 miles per hour, he'd arrive an hour before sunset and would have to sit in the heat, without even the faint breeze of his riding to cool him.

What speed does he need to travel to arrive exactly at sunset?

Solution on page 113

CHICKENS

A group of White Harbor men are meeting with a livestock merchant with the intention of buying a consignment of live chickens. Having negotiated a price that all concerned find acceptable, the men find that they have a problem dividing the cost amongst themselves evenly. If each of them pays nine pennies, they will be paying 11 pennies too much, but if each puts in six, then they have 16 pennies too little.

How many buyers are there, and what is the cost of their chickens?

Solution on page 113

A LESSON OVER DINNER

Archmaester Mollos waved his red gold rod at the novices waiting nervously in front of him and grunted disapprovingly. "You dolts seem determined to resist learning even the simplest application of numbers. So this afternoon, I have decided to give you some... encouragement.

It is my estimate that you typically manage to consume 20 spoons of food at your evening meal. Tonight, your portions will depend on your wits. The five of you will get your 100 spoons – rabbit stew, I believe it is tonight – but they will not be shared equally. The amount of food each of you gets will be staggered, decreasing by the same amount each time. The two smallest shares together will equal just one-seventh of the three collected larger shares. The first of you to tell me how many spoons each share contains will get the largest portion. The last of you will receive the smallest and I warn you now, it isn't much. Fail, and go without."

What size are the shares?

Solution on page 114

18

LISKER'S TASK

"Suppose, young Lisker, that there are 15 novices, yourself included."

"Yes, Archmaester."

"Further imagine that there is a task I have that requires a group of three novices. If I order you to change the members of your group each hour, and to progress at the task for seven hours without ever repeating the members of your group, is that possible?"

Solution on page 115

THUNDERFIST

Tormund Tall-Talker, Father of Hosts, took his title very literally. Somewhere between 50 and 80 years old, he was known to boast to have as many sons and grandsons as he had years of life. Each of his sons, so he said, had as many sons as brothers.

How old was he?

Solution on page 115

FREY TIME

A rwyn Frey's mother took her to a small manor and left her in the care of her aunt and uncle, with strict instructions to obey them in all particulars. None of her cousins were in attendance.

She was given a haircut and ordered to keep away from one entire wing. Most of the time, she was left to her own devices and her aunt and uncle were distant, at best. At other times, she was instructed to put on specific sets of clothing, sit in very precise locations in the manor and engage in various trivial pursuits with her aunt and uncle. During these periods, and these periods alone, they were extremely pleasant and sociable.

Strange noises from the forbidden wing led Arwyn to suspect that the manor was haunted, although her uncle Errik was particularly curt regarding that possibility. He was less reticent about a fellow who appeared to stalk the grounds of the manor, owning him to be a dangerous lunatic. Even so, Ser Errik made no attempt to run the man off.

Eventually, after some weeks of this, Arwyn was sent home, none the wiser. What was going on?

36

Solution on page 115

A QUIZ OF ICE AND FIRE II

1. What is Jon Snow's first assignment on the Wall?

2. Who is the master-of-arms at Castle Black when Jon Snow arrives?

3. Why is Sansa Stark's direwolf "Lady" killed?

4. Who portrays Khal Drogo in the Game of Thrones TV show?

5. Which city is the first to welcome Daenerys as The Mother Of Dragons?

6. What is the name of Theon Greyjoy's first ship?

7. Which Lord is known as the Old Man of Oldtown?

8. Who does Tywin Baratheon plan to have married to the Lord of Flowers?

9. What is the identity of Theon Greyjoy's torturer?

10. Who said "There are no true knights, no more than there are gods"?

Solution on page 116

DAENERYS'S TEA

The Braavosi maid knelt at Daenerys's feet and held up a silver tray. "Spiceflower and cinnamon tea, m'lady. There is honey to sweeten, if you like."

"Thank you." Daenerys took the cup, and sipped. Suppressing a grimace, she swiftly spooned in enough honey to make it palatable. She drank again. "Pleasant." She set the cup on the table and was about to return to her discussion when a large beetle flew past her clumsily and splashed straight into the tea.

The maid gasped and snatched the cup back. "I'm so sorry, m'lady. I will bring you more tea." She bowed again, and vanished.

A little while later, the maid returned with a fresh tea. Daernerys took a sip and frowned at the maid. "Is it your usual custom to lie to your master's guests?"

How did she know it was the same cup of tea?

Solution on page 117

DAYNE'S PARADOX

Ser Dayne smiled at Arya Stark. "I heard that you've said my fellow Dornishmen are liars, young lady. Well, let me tell you true: all Dornishmen are indeed constant liars."

"How do I know you're telling the truth?" Arya said, suspicious.

"If I'm telling you the truth then clearly I have to be lying. But if I'm lying then I'm just confirming the truth."

"It doesn't work like that," she protested.

"Oh?" Ser Dayne smiled. "How does it work then?"

Can you explain?

Solution on page 117

THE SPRAWLING

Emblem of youth and innocence,

With walls surrounded for defence,
Yet by no worldly cares oppressed,
I boldly spread my charms around,
Till some rude lover breaks the mound,
And rudely clasps me to his breast.
Here soon I sicken and decay
My beauty lost, I'm turned away.
Who am I?

Solution on page 117

A CAUTIOUS PACE

Sent by the Brotherhood on an errand, Thoros of Myr took his time on the outward journey, ambling along at a rate of four miles an hour. On his return, keen to be done with it all, he stirred himself to a more respectable six miles an hour.

What was his average speed?

Solution on page 118

A MATTER OF BIRTHDAYS

"Good evening, Ser Andar."

"Maester Hakon! It's an honour to see you here at Runestone this evening."

"Thank you, Ser. It is good to see you well. How many are you expecting at this gathering?"

"I believe there will be 23 of us."

"Twenty-three. That is a most interesting number. I wonder if you know the chance, at a gathering of 23, that two of those present will have been born on the same day of the year?"

"Ah…"

What's the chance?

Solution on page 118

A HUNT FOR WORDS II

```
M  R  Q  A  J  B  B  A  R  C  E  L  Z  G  R
L  S  R  E  W  O  T  E  E  R  H  T  N  O  F
E  S  H  A  D  D  N  M  A  H  O  O  Y  Y  F
N  A  G  G  S  E  N  O  T  S  I  R  T  L  S
N  R  Y  M  I  R  H  N  S  A  P  R  G  E  E
O  Y  E  G  E  A  M  D  R  Q  L  H  R  E  A
D  A  M  M  E  J  H  A  I  R  Y  E  S  T  S
C  W  K  D  A  T  H  Q  F  X  N  N  A  S  M
S  A  Y  L  E  N  R  A  A  A  S  S  N  Q  O
R  A  V  G  O  A  D  Y  H  F  O  S  V  O  K
J  Y  R  E  V  O  C  O  O  A  C  Q  I  R  E
N  L  L  Y  D  N  A  R  N  L  U  U  L  G  G
W  I  L  L  E  M  L  E  K  Y  L  A  R  Y  S
R  O  N  I  L  E  A  Q  C  S  X  R  L  L  M
F  I  J  Y  Y  U  U  X  J  E  C  E  X  E  V
```

AELINOR	FALYSE	KDATH	RORGE
AEMOND	FIRST	LARYS	SARYA
ALVYN	FORLEY	LUCOS	SEA SMOKE
ANVIL	GOADY	MAEGE	SHADD
COVER	HAIGH	MANDON	STEELY
CRABB	HAIRY	MEJHAH	TALEA
DONNEL	HOARE	OLYVAR	THREE TOWERS
EDMYN	JARED	PRYOR	TORRHEN'S SQUARE
ELYAS	JAYDE	QORGYLE	TRISTON
ERENA	JONOS	RANDYLL	WILLEM

Solution on page 119

AGE OF AMBROSE

"So you see, Ser Jason, in seven years time, my and Alyssane's combined ages will be 64 years."

"Arthur is quite right, Lord Mallister. When he were the age that I am now, he was twice as old as I was then."

What ages are the Ambroses?

Solution on page 120

THE MALLISTERS

Fascinating, Ser Arthur. Alys and I also have an interesting confluence of our ages, as it happens. Her age and mine use the same numbers, but reversed, and the difference between our ages is but an eleventh of their total."

"I am definitely younger than Jason however, Lord Ambrose."

What ages are the Mallisters?

Solution on page 120

TANNER

Wattle had been apprenticed to Maise the Tanner for six months. Even by the high standards of Reeking Lane, tanning was a foul and dangerous business but the lad was keen to make a good impression. Dunking skins into an acid bath one afternoon, and watching the level of the liquid rise within its tub, he found himself wondering if it might not be possible to save money. Anything that meant using less acid would be an improvement in his life, as well.

A much wider rod, he reasoned, would take up more space in the bath, so the acid would rise higher and treat more of the skin lashed to it. Then, of course, he realized that the bath would need to be higher, to stop the acid spilling. But the rods would be taking up space there as well and the acid would rise higher still, and if he made the bath higher yet, the rods would still be there, and no matter how high he made the tub…

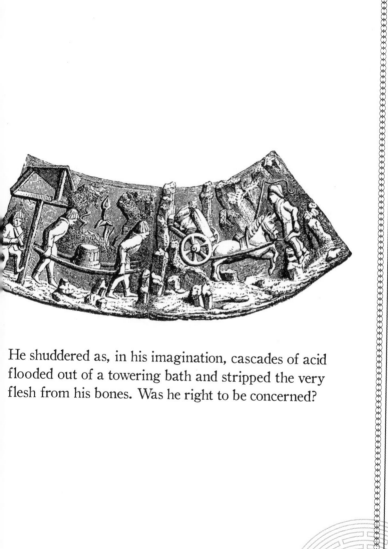

He shuddered as, in his imagination, cascades of acid flooded out of a towering bath and stripped the very flesh from his bones. Was he right to be concerned?

Solution on page 121

THREE BOXES

A rchmaester Mollos placed three small boxes on the table before him, and looked up at the novices assembled before him. "Three boxes," he declared. "Each one holds two small bags and each bag contains a single coin. In one box, there are two gold dragons. In another, two silver stags. In the third, one dragon and one stag. I do not remember which box holds which coins. You, Hobb, come here, and take a bag from one of the boxes."

Nervously, the novice did as he was told.

"Good. Now, what coin is inside?"

Hobb opened the bag. "A dragon, sir."

"Fine. Now, which of you dolts can tell me what the chance is that the other coin in that same box is also a gold dragon?"

Solution on page 121

SER GLADDEN

"Ser Gladden, how old are you?"

"A bold question, child. In six years time, I will be one-and-a-quarter the age I was four years ago."

How old is Ser Gladden?

Solution on page 122

SIX BARRELS

The landlord of the Inn at the Crossroads, Masha Heddle, purchased six barrels of unusually good wine from a vintner. One was of a vintage significantly better than the rest and that she kept for herself. The others, still sealed, went to two customers, one of whom bought twice as many pints of wine as the other. Each barrel held a different amount and their sizes were 15 pints, 16 pints, 18 pints, 19 pints, 20 pints and 31 pints.

Which barrel was the one that Masha kept for herself?

Solution on page 123

THE WOODSMAN

When three farms were robbed in as many days by a tall, muscular, weathered-looking fellow with a big nose and a huge beard, the House Leygood guards were immediately suspicious that the beard had been used as a way of throwing them off the villain's trail. After a little investigation, they found a heap of trimmed facial hair not far from the third victim's home.

Suspicion fell on a local woodsman, named Crom. He was of the right build, depth of tan and nasal prominence, and was now clean-shaven, despite several villagers remembering him as being bearded six months before. He insisted that he was innocent and that he had removed his beard four months prior, following a nasty incident with woodlice, a bottle of spirits and an open bonfire.

Sentiment quickly turned against him, however, and it was looking bleak until a Leygood guardsman with more wits than usual pointed out an element of Crom's appearance that ruled him out beyond any doubt. What was it?

Solution on page 123

THE BIG ADVENTURE

GERIS CHARLTON

Geris Charlton was often heard to boast that he had twice as many sisters as brothers, while his twin sister Gerra had just as many brothers as sisters. Eventually, his aunt Berenia pointed out that his cousin Leystone had three times as many sisters as brothers, while Leystone's sister Rhee still had just as many brothers as sisters.

Who had the more brothers, Geris or Leystone?

Solution on page 126

A TRAY OF CAKES

At Winterfell, Gage had baked three batches of apple cakes. Each batch was slightly different – the first had added blueberries, the second contained pine-nuts and the third featured chopped prunes. When the batches were finished, he put them aside carefully, in the order of their cooking, so he'd know which was which.

To his annoyance, when he returned to the apple cakes, one of the other cooks had shifted the platters around so that none of them were in the correct position. Given his reluctance to waste his work, what is the fewest number of apple cakes he would have to cut open to find out the identities of each platter?

Solution on page 126

57

BUTTERWELL

Family relationships can swiftly get tangled, even in the Riverlands. Perla is Shay's third cousin once removed, on her mother's side. What relation is Perla's grandmother to Shay's son?

Solution on page 126

INFINITE REALMS

"Play close attention to this, Frey."

"Yes, Archmaester Mollos."

"Start with a number and add one to it. How far can you keep going, getting ever-larger numbers?"

"Forever, sir."

"Quite. Now, start with the same original number and add two to it. Again how far can you keep going?"

"Well, it would be forever again."

"Exactly. So riddle me this, young Robert. Collect up all the numbers you count, in both those sequences. Which of the sequences is larger?"

Solution on page 127

A QUIZ OF ICE AND FIRE II

1. Why does Ned Stark try to resign as Hand of the King?

2. Who is known as The Spider?

3. What is odd about the raven in Bran Stark's dreams?

4. Alfie Allen, who plays Theon Greyjoy in the Game of Thrones TV show is the brother of which musical artist?

5. Who leads the defence of the Mud Gate at the battle of Blackwater?

6. Who is named Savior of King's Landing?

7. Who leads the Faith of the Seven?

8. How did Maester Qyburn lose his chain?

9. How does Lord Rickard Karstark die?

10. What is Hag's Teeth?

Solution on page 128

A HUNT FOR WORDS III

```
M A E R I E S M A R W Y L L A
A Y J D L T E K E L R U K A A
C C L D J V A R D I S N R N D
O Y J E G D U M E F K K Y O O
R X Y D S T E P C N U A W D O
N N Z N L R E B M O L I O H W
E D M U N D N L A N L Y L A N
E S V O B O M M U L P P L D O
T Y Z S D N N S F C L D I N R
A E N A R R K O U L A E W A Y
E L L L O C K E L T O S Y R D
R E H T A E W Y R R E M E R B
G M S L T O R G O N A L Y U D
N E B B I K N Y W E L M C R P
N A M O W G N I P E E W F W K
```

ACORN	JEYNE	MUDGE	SOUND
AENAR	KURLEKET	MYLES	TORGON
BLACK	LAYNA	NESTOR	VARDIS
CLETUS	LEWYN	OMBER	VULTURE
DONAL	LOCKE	PLUMM	WALDA
EDMUND	LUCAS	RANDA	WEEPING WOMAN
ELADON	MAERIE	RENLY	WILLOW
ELLERY	MARLON	RYELLA	WYLLA
GREAT	MELEYS	RYMOLF	YRONWOOD
IBBEN	MERRYWEATHER	SKULL	YUNKAI

Solution on page 129

DAARIO AND THE GREY WORM

Daario Naharis and the Grey Worm found themselves in so heated an argument that the Worm was in danger of considering raising his voice a little – and all over the matter of a game.

"You're being a blind, obstinate fool," Daario yelled. He made a Herculean effort to calm himself. "It is clearly easier to roll at least three sixes from 18 dice-tosses than it is to get at least one six from six tosses. There are so many more chances."

The Grey Worm shook his head politely. "You are incorrect. It is the other way around."

Who is correct?

Solution on page 130

42

KHALEESI OF THORNS

"**W**hat has Lady Olenna got for us today?"

"She wants to walk down to the Mander," Arryk said.

Erryk sighed. "Walk? Gods, why?"

"Who knows? Watch the boats, maybe."

"It'll take an age. Three miles an hour downhill to get there maybe, but one mile an hour back uphill."

"You had something else to do with those six hours?" asked Arryk. "It's not as if we have to jog."

"I suppose not."

Lady Olenna's screech came from the other room. "Left! Right! Come here."

"Here we go again," Erryk said.

How far is the journey?

Solution on page 130

QARTH

Xaro Xhoan Daxos turned the parchment over thoughtfully. It had been delivered by a slave but bore no identifying signature or seal. The message was short, and if it was a threat then it was a particularly oblique and subtle one.

In a beautiful, flowing hand, the message read, "A stack and its seventh together reach 19."

There was nothing more. Try as he might, Xaro could discern no purpose in the message.

How big is the stack?

Solution on page 131

TWO TWINS

Two twins we are and there is no surprise,

That we're alike in feature, shape, and size.
We're often round, of brass or iron made,
Or mayhaps wood, yet useful still in trade.
But even so, for all our daily pains,
We by the neck are often hung in chains.
What are we?

Solution on page 131

BRIDGER CERWYN

"Did you hear, Andar? When Lord Medger's father, Bridger Cerwyn, married his current wife, 18 years ago, he was three times as old as Beedie, his bride."

"So what?"

"So now, he's just twice as old as she is."

"Well how old was he, then, when they married?"

Solution on page 131

MEN WITHOUT HATS

Three separate men were sitting in the Red Dome coffee house in central Braavos. The first, Gergen, was cautiously watching the door. The second, Barth, was just as cautiously watching Gergen. The third, Mudge, was being even more careful about watching Barth. One of the things that Barth noted was that Gergen had long, slightly greasy hair that held a faint scent of offal. Mudge, unobserved as he was by either man, was as hairlessly bald as it was possible for a man to become.

Given that Barth's baldness or hairiness was unrecorded, can you tell whether, amongst the three, there was a bald man looking at a hairy man?

Solution on page 132

THE GREAT OTHER

A small stir arose in the Temple of the Lord of Light in Volantis when a long-forgotten prophecy attributed to a priest of the Great Other was discovered on Crackclaw Point. The prophecy warned that a circle of adepts of the Great Other should be maintained at all times, lest ruin result. The priests of R'hllor immediately started working to uncover the full import of the scroll.

One of the prophecy's clearer sections described the number that had to form the circle – seven blind, to see behind the light; three blind in one eye, to see both light and shade; five with normal vision, to perceive the truth; and nine who see through one eye, for focus and purity.

What are the maximum and minimum sizes of the circle of adepts?

Solution on page 132

VALAR MORGHULIS

Ser Normon Wythers was in his library, working. His wife, Cerenda, was in her own rooms in the keep when she heard raised voices from the library. Her husband, sounding concerned, was talking to an angry-sounding man with a rough voice. She couldn't make out the words, but the argument intensified until she heard a horrible scream, followed by a nasty thud, and silence.

Cerenda was already standing at the library door and trying it nervously, found it locked. Her screams fetched guards, who battered the door down and found Ser Norman dead, with a plain-looking dagger through his heart. The library windows were high above the ground but even so, they were intact and tightly latched on the inside. There were no other ways in or out of the room and no place where an intruder could have remained hidden.

Lady Cerenda admitted that her husband had been preoccupied for several weeks but he had given her no reason to believe that he was in danger. A maester was called and he was able to state with confidence that there was no supernatural element involved in Ser Normon's fate.

So what happened?

Solution on page 133

PLAYING THE FIELD

Braganthos Woodwright was set upon making a grand gesture to impress Margaery Tyrell and he hit upon the idea of a very particular field. His plan was to make an enclosure for jousting and archery but to elevate it above all other fields, it would be perfectly square and surrounded by a barred wooden fence. The fence would be seven bars high at all points, to honour the gods, and would surround an area of exactly as many acres as there were bars. The wooden bars he selected for this endeavour were each 2.75 yards in length. For reference, you should probably know than one acre is 4,840 square yards, which you could consider as being equivalent to 55 x 88 yards.

What size will the field be?

Solution on page 133

ALLYCE & WILLIT

"**H**a ha, Willitt. I was behind you!"

"No way, Rolf. I was behind you!"

"No! I'm right!"

"No you're not! I'm right!"

Allyce sighed. "Quiet down, you two. You're both right."

How?

Solution on page 133

THE PLANK

As Wat watched, his master, Desmon, sawed a thick plank into chunks. First of all, he sawed it precisely in half, then he fastened the pieces together and sawed them both in half. Finally, he gathered up all four chunks, and sawed them in half once more. Wiping dust off himself, Desmon grabbed one of the small pieces of wood, and tossed it across to Wat.

Wat looked at it doubtfully. "That was a 20-pound plank."

Desmon nodded.

"So this weighs, uh, two-and-a-half pounds," said Wat.

Desmon spat on the floor. "Nope."

Where has Wat gone wrong?

Solution on page 134

LAZY LEO

A colyte Tyrell was somewhat startled when he rounded a corner in the Citadel to find Archmaester Mollos just standing there in front of him. He was even more startled when Mollos flourished a pair of envelopes at him. A hoarse "Sir?" was the best he could manage.

The old man glared at him. "One of these envelopes, acolyte, contains a credit slip for one silver stag. The other contains a slip for two silver stags. Pick one."

"Uh…"

"Pick one, or receive none, acolyte."

Tyrell snatched one hastily.

"So. This remaining envelope either has half as much value as the one you've chosen, or twice as much. You may exchange the one you have. Does it make sense to swap?"

Thinking furiously, Tyrell said, "Well, if I make the wrong choice I only lose half, but if I make the right choice, I gain the same again. That means the potential profit is double the potential risk. So yes, it makes sense."

"Very well," said Mollos. He swapped Tyrell's envelope. "Now, I ask you the same question. Does it make sense to swap?"

Tyrell's face fell. "Well yes… Ah."

What is wrong with his logic?

Solution on page 134

A QUIZ OF ICE AND FIRE IV

1. What title does Robb Stark claim when the North secedes from the Seven Kingdoms?

2. What document does Cersei Lannister tear up before ordering Ned Stark arrested?

3. Where does King Robert Baratheon appoint Ned Stark as his Hand?

4. Who does Aidan Gillen play in the Game of Thrones TV show?

5. What is Mance Rayder's title?

6. Who orders Davos Seaworth to denounce Cersei's children as illegitimate to the whole of the Seven Kingdoms?

7. Where are the best far-eyes made?

8. What price does Daenerys Targaryen pay for the Unsullied?

9. What is Ser Brynden Tully's nickname?

10. Who had a horse called Glory?

Solution on page 135

A HUNDRED GEMS

In Pentos, Illyrio came into a consignment of opals, which he decided to convert into livestock. He called one of his bronze-collared servants and gave the man 100 gems, with strict instructions to exchange them entirely for exactly 100 animals. The beasts he wanted were camels, at five opals each, asses at one opal each, and goats at 20 per opal, and at least one of each.

How many of each animal did the servant return with?

Solution on page 136

79

PEARLS OF WISDOM

" Look at this pair of bags, novice. There is an identically sized stone in each bag, in each case either a bead or a pearl, with an even chance of each. Between them, the bags may hold two beads, two pearls, or one of each. Now, this pearl goes into the second bag, which is refastened. Pay attention. I shake that bag, and draw out... a pearl. So be it. Now both bags hold one stone again. Which bag – if either – is now more likely to be holding a pearl?"

Solution on page 136

GOLD AND GREEN

Ser Dunstad Westbrook was a fair man by nature. So when he was called on to adjudicate the terms of a rather obscure will left by a wealthy merchant, he was determined to do his best.

The deceased man wanted his sons to have gold squares commemorating their father. The gold square of the younger son had to have sides three-quarters the length of the square going to the elder son. For this purpose, the man had set aside enough gold to cover 100 square inches, at an even thickness of ¼-inch".

The issue that nobody could quite seem to settle on was the size of the two squares. How long should their sides be?

Solution on page 136

81

AS THE RAVEN FLIES

Travelling from Longtable to Ashford, it is possible to get diverted by heading instead to Cider Hall and from there completing your journey. Cider Hall is nearer to Longtable than Ashford is but it sits 12 miles from the road to Ashford. That indirect route is 35 miles. If all the roads are straight, how far is the direct route from Longtable to Ashford?

Solution on page 137

THE DAWN'S DELAY

I was here before the world began,
and shall forever last.

Born before the rivers ran, in dim
and distant past.

Your youthful moments I attend
and mitigate your grief;

The industrious peasant I
befriend, and to victims bring
relief.

Make much of me if you are
wise and use me while you may,

For you will find that in a
trice, you too I'll come to slay.

Who am I?

Solution on page 137

REDFORT

Finding them together in a quiet moment, young Mychel darted up to his parents. "How old are you, mother?"

Lady Houtella blinked at the sudden interruption. "If you add your age, and mine, and your father's, it comes to precisely 70 years, with no months left over."

"That's a lot," said Mychel. "And how old are you, father?"

"Six times your age," said Lord Horton.

Mychel frowned. "So when will I be just half your age, then?"

"When that happens, our three ages will be double the total that they are today."

"But..."

"But now it's time for bed," Lady Houtella said firmly.

How old are the Redforts?

Solution on page 138

RAYDER'S TOWER

Val the wildling came to the defence of a pair of children who'd offended the wildling warlord Mance Rayder, and almost before she knew it, she found herself locked with them in a tower of punishment, out in the deep woods. The tower was ice-clad, and nigh-impossible to climb, but it did have a pair of baskets linked by a pulley so that food could be provided. Getting into a basket without a strong counterweight would be disastrous – a 15lb disparity between basket loads was the most that a human could risk if trying to travel in a basket. She weighed a muscular 175lb, while Stig and Ynga weighed 95lb and 80lb respectively. After some thought, she made a big bundle of the fuel, food, water and furs in their cell, along with some chunks of hearthstone. When the bundle reached 65lb, she declared herself satisfied, and proceeded to get herself and the children down from the tower.

How?

Solution on page 138

FAIR ISLE

Ser Gareth Clifton was very particular about his will. Amongst his many bequests, he was particularly concerned about his wine cellar, which he wanted to share evenly amongst his five sons. He had 45 casks of fine wine that he wished to see distributed. Nine of them held four gallons, nine more held three gallons, a further nine held two gallons, another nine held one gallon, and the final nine were empty five-galloners, but still of value as well-seasoned casks.

How can he make sure that each son gets an identical volume of wine (18 gallons) and number of casks (nine), while still receiving at least one of each volume of cask?

Solution on page 139

LADIES, NOT IN WAITING

When he entered the ballroom of the Red Keep, Tytos immediately noticed a group of lovely ladies talking together at a nearby table, including a couple of his acquaintance. Putting on his most charming smile, he sauntered over to them, and grandly declared, "Ten pretty maids, all in a row! By the Gods, I never did think to see such beauty."

Lady Marissa arched her eyebrow. "I'm afraid you seem to be badly mistaken, Ser Tytos. I'm afraid we are neither in a row, nor ten in number. However, I do suppose that if we were twice as many again as we are, we would of necessity be as far above ten so gathered as we presently are below it."

"Ug," Tytos said, thoroughly taken aback. "Um, thank you." With that he left, trying to ignore the giggles coming from behind him.

How many women are in the group?

Solution on page 139

SER ONDRE

Ser Ondre had sent the new recruits to the Hellholt House Guard on a training run – 15 miles through the Dornish desert, with just one flask of water (and no resupply allowed), departing an hour before noon. First man back would win lighter duties for a week.

As Arrone fought his way back to the keep, throat as dry as the dust he was caked in, he saw another man sitting on the ground. Enrike looked dreadful, pale and panting, drenched in sweat. Ser Ondre stood over him, sternly. As Enrike finally caught his breath, Ser Ondre unleashed a torrent of the most hideously vile abuse at him, concluding with a month of punishment detail.

Arrone flinched as Ser Ondre turned to him, but the man merely nodded, and told him to go get refreshed.

What had Enrike done wrong?

Solution on page 140

A HUNT FOR WORDS IV

```
C  I  L  E  W  R  Y  V  R  C  H  T  A  A  S
M  A  W  L  L  I  H  R  E  V  L  I  S  S  W
I  A  R  E  R  Y  L  E  S  E  U  E  H  O  K
G  L  T  C  N  E  L  L  A  I  R  O  O  S  E
O  S  L  R  O  D  D  E  N  L  R  D  Y  S  T
W  Y  V  V  Y  I  S  E  R  S  E  S  C  R  H  T
E  W  F  J  R  C  A  L  A  D  M  W  G  P  E
N  L  Z  E  K  I  E  Y  H  L  J  I  O  A  R
A  E  B  A  K  E  O  E  S  A  L  R  T  R  V
R  M  A  E  T  C  A  S  A  D  O  A  S  S  D
U  Q  E  A  N  W  I  G  M  Y  R  P  E  T  E
A  L  L  I  S  Y  T  R  B  A  E  Y  R  A  L
F  S  A  M  O  L  A  E  L  F  N  P  O  N  D
T  O  O  F  G  N  I  D  D  U  P  S  F  I  O
H  O  S  T  E  E  N  S  L  Y  N  T  E  N  N
```

ALLARD	GOWEN	NELLA	SLATE
ARSTAN	HOSTEEN	PUDDINGFOOT	SLYNT
AURANE	ILLYRIOS MANSE	PYPAR	SWORD
BAELA	KETTER	RODDEN	ULRICK
CARCOSA	LIGHT	ROOSE	UMBER
CLEOS	LOMAS	RYLES	VEILED LADY
DAYNE	LOREN	SAATH	VYRWEL
ELDON	MASHA	SANSA	WENDEL
ESGRED	MATRICE	SHORE	WOODS
FOREST	MELWYS	SILVERHILL	YSILLA

Solution on page 141

A FOOL'S GAME

"**M**aester Lomys! Maester Lomys!"

Lomys turned to see Highgarden's fool, Butterbumps, bearing down on him. He shuddered lightly. "What is it?"

The fool grinned. "I have a game for you, Maester."

"I hardly think…"

"Oh, but you'll like this. I have collected a basket of 50 potatoes. I will lay them out in a straight line, increasingly far apart. The first two are just one yard from each other. The third is three yards from the second. The fourth is five yards from the third. And so on. Your part is to collect them again, one at a time, an gather them in a heap by the first potato."

Lomys stared at the jester coldly. "I can hardly accuse you of having lost your wits, given that foolishness and flatulence comprise your entire purpose, but you'll have to search elsewhere for victims. Perhaps Ser Vortimer can lend you a dullard to torment. Shoo. Bedevil someone else."

How far would Lomys have to walk to collect the fool's potatoes?

Solution on page 142

BREA'S FEAST

Brea the cook watched Maester Tallan twitch nervously, and mutter to himself. Eventually, she went over to him to find out was ailing the old fellow.

"A troublesome dinner to arrange, mistress Brea," the man replied.

"No matter to me," she assured him. "However many as is coming, I'll feed 'em."

"I'm sure, I'm sure," Tallan said. "But the protocol! Ser Buford is hosting his brother's father-in-law, his father-in-law's brother, his father's brother-in-law and his brother-in-law's father."

"What of it?" asked Brea, mystified. "It's just four guests."

Maester Tallen threw his hands in the air. "No, no! That would be the most Ser Buford could be expecting. But he has invited just the very least!"

Brea frowned. "How many is that, then?"

Solution on page 142

GOODBROOK

When Ser Goodbrook died, his will instructed that his eldest son should receive half of his beloved herd of stallions. One-third of the herd was to go to the middle son, and one-ninth to the youngest. Unfortunately, at that time, Ser Goodbrook's herd numbered 17 horses, and his sons could see no way to divide the herd up as requested without dividing one or more horses into bloody chunks.

When they discussed the matter with the stable master, he was able to fix the matter – at no personal loss to himself – so that it was possible to share the herd fairly between the brothers without killing any horses, and without involving any fifth parties.

How can this be done?

Solution on page 142

SIMEON STAR-EYES

They say that Symeon Star-Eyes was so skilled that given a target 40 feet away, he could fire an arrow straight through his hat every time he tried.

"They do, do they? That's not difficult, you fool. Give me a minute with old Blind Pew and I'll have him doing the same ten times in a row."

"Nonsense. Old Pew hasn't held a bow in 30 years and even then he couldn't hit a chicken in a henyard. Star-Eyes was a mighty hero!"

"A gold dragon says I'm right."

What's the way to do it?

Solution on page 143

THE DOOR'S GUARD

What force and strength cannot get through,

I with a gentle touch can do,

And many in the streets would stand,

Were I not right
there at hand.

What am I?

Solution on page 143

BAQQ

The Windblown known as Beans was fond of dice, and during a dull hour at the siege of Astapor he concocted a new game to inflict upon his comrades. Taking a board, he divided it into six sections and numbered them from one to six. Then he invited his friends to bet on a particular number to come up on the throw of three dice. Anyone who picked a number that showed on any of the three dice would get their stake back, plus the same again for each dice that showed that number. So, for example, betting on 'four' for a roll of four, two, four would return your original wager, plus twice as much again.

As a player, what is the chance of winning at this game?

Solution on page 143

THE QUEST
ANSWERS

KIRRA'S APPLES

"A number plus its quarter" indicates that 5/4 of the solution equals 15, so the answer is 15 x 4/5, or 12 barrels.

SQUARED SERS

Ser Manfryd is 39, his wife is 34, his son is 14 and his daughter is 13. Ser Raynard is 42, his wife is 40, his son is 10 and his daughter is eight.

FOWLER PLAY

If one is lying, the other must also be lying.
Jeyne is on the right, and Jennelyn on the left.

OLD WYK

The trick is to empty the central cell of each row. Nine
acolytes can then be split between the corner cells at
the end of that row however you please – so long as the
parallel row has its corner cells filled in the opposite
manner. So you could arrange, say, nine acolytes at top left
and none at top right, then none again at bottom left and
nine at bottom right.

THE MAESTER'S HAND

In part, the air actually is cooler when blown quickly, because expanding from the tight stream you force it into reduces its temperature a little. Mainly however, a stream of air evaporates moisture from your skin, cooling it, and this effect happens more swiftly when the air is moving faster.

DRAGONSTONE

Two widows married each others' sons, and each new union brought forth a daughter. These six lie inside.

LORD DAERON VAITH

If Gage is telling the truth, then Rafe also has to be telling the truth, and he claims Gage is lying, so it can't be him. If Rafe is telling the truth, then Gage is also telling the truth, so again, it can't be him. So Alarn has to be telling the truth.

A QUIZ OF
ICE AND FIRE I

1. Theon Greyjoy

2. Tysha

3. Ser Jorah Mormont

4. With onions and salt fish

5. Daenerys Targaryen

6. Riverrun

7. Tyrion Lannister

8. Sandor the Hound

9. Lannister

10. Jaqen H'ghar

VARYS

A mole.

FAIRMARKET

A hundred bushels of barley with 8 percent chaff is 92 bushels of pure barley. To sift 92 bushels of pure barley from a mix that was one-third chaff, you'd need half as much chaff as there was pure barley (two-thirds to one-third), or 138 bushels.

HOUSE MARTELL

They are four generations of the same family,
father to son. Petyr is Harlen's father. Harlen is
Theodore's father.
Theodore is Selmont's father.

THE BAY OF CRABS

As the last quarter equals the third quarter, and the last
half equals the first half, then the runners hit the
three-quarter mark exactly three-quarters of the way
through the race.
6.75 ÷ 3 = 2.25, and 2.25 x 4 = 9 minutes.

FIRST IMPRESSIONS

Dragons – take the first letter of each line.

```
R N N W O T S Y A W O R R A H
H E A R T E A T E R V Y J M R
W V L N S H E L B Q L G N B H
E E A W O J G Y L I M Y Y E L
D S S W Q E X R Q A O G T R L
Y E E K R F T N E Q R E L L O
T H R G S W I J D E L I N Y R
K T E N N J R P S Y N X A V Q
C N S H E L D K M L A N S A
A R E Y F N Y M E R I A W N M
L O D A F Y K H A D O K H A A
B B J F A J F O R A X M K Y
N E F E R J Y H T N I L F E I
G R I G G Q N U G V U Y Q S X
S T K G S A R G O N I V A C M
```

DORNISH TROUBLE

t (obviously) takes one hour to travel ten miles at 10mph, and two-thirds of an hour to travel ten miles at 15mph. We need a distance that gives a two-hour gap between the two speeds. The difference for ten miles between the two speeds is a third of an hour, so we need six lots of that difference, or 60 miles. Sixty miles is six hours at 10mph, and that's an hour too late, so sunset is five hours away. That means the speed required to travel 60 miles in five hours is $60 \div 5 = 12$mph.

CHICKENS

If 'x' is the number of buyers, 9x is 11 too much, and 6x is 16 too little. Looking at the difference, that means $3x = 27$, so x, the number of buyers, is 9. We know the value is 11 less than 9 times x, so the value is 81–11. There are nine men, paying 70 pennies between them.

A LESSON OVER DINNER

If you approach this puzzle methodically, it's actually quite straightforward. First, you need to work out the size of the gap between shares that gives you the right ratio of $(A + B + C) \div 7 = (D + E)$. First, try it with just sequential numbers. $(5 + 4 + 3) \div 7 = 1.71$, which is 1.29 away from $(2 + 1) = 3$. Fine. Now try a simple increase in the sequence gaps. $(9 + 7 + 5) \div 7 = 3$, which is one away from $(3 + 1) = 4$. That's good, we've gotten $2/7$ closer to a difference of zero by increasing the gap between numbers by one. The difference is one, or $7/7$, so we try increasing the gap between numbers by 3.5 $(7/2)$, to 5.5. This gives us 1, 6.5, 12, 17.5 and 23. 1 + 6.5 = 7.5; and 12 + 17.5 + 23 = 52.5, where $52.5 \div 7 = 7.5$. That's the right ratio. The five numbers together total up to 60 though, not 100, so we need to multiply our numbers by $100 \div 60$, or 1.667. So, our final breakdown of shares, from largest to smallest, is 38.33 spoons, 29.17 spoons, 20 spoons, 10.83 spoons and 1.67 spoons, where $(38.33 + 29.17 + 20) = 87.5$, and $(87.5/7) = (10.83 + 1.67) = 12.5$, and $87.5 + 12.5 = 100$.

This method of solving problems by putting in a series of wrong solutions and seeing how the answer changes is known as *Regula Falsi*.

LISKER'S TASK

Indeed it is. Fifteen novices means Lisker plus 14 others, so there's enough people for him to work with two others each hour without repeating.

THUNDERFIST

His age – the total of his sons and grandsons – has to be a square number if each son has as many brothers as sons. 64 is the only square number between 50 and 80.

FREY TIME

Arwyn was being used to stand in for one of her cousins, who had been carrying on a relationship with the supposed lunatic. Her parents, disapproving of their love, had locked their daughter in the forbidden wing and made Arwen up to look like her. They then feigned cheerful family life as a charade for the suitor, to try to convince him that their daughter had forgotten him entirely and was carrying on with life as usual without him. It didn't work, so they gave up and sent Arwyn home.

A QUIZ OF
ICE AND FIRE II

1. Steward to the Lord Commander

2. Alliser Thorne

3. Because her sister's direwolf ran away after biting Joffrey Baratheon

4. Jason Momoa

5. Qarth

6. The Sea Bitch

7. Lord (Leyton) Hightower

8. His daughter, Cersei

9. Ramsay Snow, the Bastard of Bolton

10. Sandor Clegane, The Hound

DAENERYS'S TEA

The tea was exactly as sweet as it was before.

DAYNE'S PARADOX

There are a couple of common "solutions" to the Liars Paradox. Ser Dayne can be lying without that proving that all Dornishmen are liars. Say, for example, he lies, but his mother is scrupulously honest. Then he's simply lying and there's no paradox. Similarly, there would be no reason to assume every Dornishman lies all the time, so again, Ser Dayne's lie does not prove anything. For an alternative approach, he may simply be wrong about the matter, and so telling an incorrect "truth".

THE SPRAWLING

A rose.

A CAUTIOUS PACE

Because Thoros spends less time travelling at a higher speed, the average is not midway between the two speeds. Let's say it's a 24-mile journey. Then, at 4mph, it will take six hours there. Similarly, at 6mph, returning will take four hours. So Thoros will have travelled 24 x 2 = 48 miles in exactly ten hours. 48 ÷ 10 = 4.8mph. This average will be the same for any distance.

A MATTER OF BIRTHDAYS

Because the number of links between people increases very swiftly as group size grows, in fact there is slightly better than a 50 percent chance that any two people in a group of 23 will have the same birthday. (To be exact, it is 50.7 percent, and you get a 99 percent chance with a group of 57 people).

A HUNT FOR WORDS II

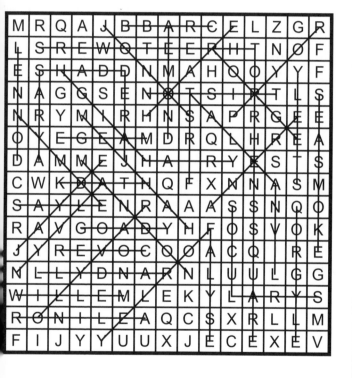

M R Q A J B B A R C E L Z G R
L S R E W O T E E R H T N O F
E S H A D D N M A H O O Y Y F
N A G G S E N O T S I I T L S
N R Y M I R H N S A P R G E E
O Y E G E A M D R Q L H R E A
D A M M E J H A I R Y X S T S
C W K B A T H Q F X N N A S M
S A Y L E N R A A A S S N Q O
R A V G O A D Y H F O S V O K
J Y R E V O C O O A C Q I R E
N L L Y D N A R N L U U L G G
W I L L E M L E K Y L A R Y S
R O N I L E A Q C S X R L L M
F I J Y Y U U X J E C E X E V

AGE OF AMBROSE

If they are going to be 64 in seven years, then their current total age is 50. If her current age is twice her previous age, then his current age has to be three times her previous age (because it's twice her previous age, plus her previous age again). So he is 30, and she is 20, and when he was 20, she was ten.

THE MALLISTERS

When you add complimentary numbers together – such as 12 + 21 – you always get a multiple of 11. The smallest gap between such numbers is nine, when the two digits of the numbers are sequential, again as in 12 and 21. 9 x 11 gives 99, and the only pair of numbers that fit the pattern and total 99 are 45 and 54, which are the ages of Alys and Jason Mallister respectively.

TANNER

No. Provided that the rod is smaller than the tub – which it has to be to fit inside – there will always be a height beyond which the acid will not rise. This will vary according to the diameter of the tub and the rod, but it can certainly be calculated in advance.

THREE BOXES

The answer is ⅔. Intuitively, most people feel that the box was either G/S or G/G, which means there is either G or S left, so the answer is ½. However, you have twice as much chance to pick a first gold coin from the G1/G2 box as you do from the G/S box, so the fact that you've already picked a gold coin means it's more likely that you have the G1/G2 box selected than the G/S box. Mathematically, you have three possibilities that start with a gold coin being selected – pick G, leaving S; or pick G1, leaving G2; or pick G2, leaving G1. Two of those three possibilities end with a second gold coin.

SER GLADDEN

Let's call Gladden's current age "x".
Mathematically, his statement breaks down to $(x + 6) = (x - 4) \times \frac{5}{4}$. Multiply both sides by four to get rid of the divisor, so $4x + 24 = (x-4) \times 5 = 5x - 20$. Now add that 20 to both sides. $4x + 44 = 5x$. Finally, subtract the $4x$ from both sides, and $44 = x$. Ser Gladden is 44, and in six years time, he'd be 50, which is one and a quarter times 40, his age four years ago.

SIX BARRELS

We know that we need to add all the barrels to a total divisible by three with one left over. The total of all six is 119. That's not divisible by three, so removing 15 or 18 would be no help. Further more, 119 is two above 117, the previous number divisible by three, so subtracting a number that is just one above being divisible by three – i.e. 31, 19 and 16 – is also no use. The only barrel that is two numbers above a multiple of three is 20, so that is the beer. Remove that and you have 99 left, divided into 66 to one man and 33 to the other.

THE WOODSMAN

Crom is tanned, but if he had shaved off a huge beard a few days before, his cheeks, neck and jaw would be significantly paler than the rest of him.

THE BIG ADVENTURE
ANSWERS

GERIS CHARLTON

Geris does. He has two brothers and four sisters, while Leystone has one brother and three sisters.

A TRAY OF CAKES

One trial is sufficient if each type is in the wrong position. Consider the cakes as A, B and C. If type C is in position A, then since position B cannot hold type B, it must hold type A, leaving the missing type B in position C. Similar logic holds for B being in place A.

BUTTERWELL

According to the described relationship, Shay's great-grandmother was the sister of Perla's great-great-grandmother. Perla's grandmother and Shay's mother were thus second cousins, as their grandmothers were sisters. This means that Perla's grandmother would be second cousin twice removed to Shay's son.

INFINITE REALMS

It's a trick question. As it turns out, the term "larger" is mostly meaningless when you start working with infinity. On the one hand, there are obviously twice as many whole numbers as there are even whole numbers. On the other hand, two things which extend to infinity are both the same size – infinite. With all that said though, modern science generally considers the two to be the same order of magnitude (known as Aleph Zero), even though their precise sizes are considered incalculable. We don't have room here, but check out the work of the mathematician Georg Cantor for a look at how startlingly beautiful the mathematics of infinity can become.

A QUIZ OF
ICE AND FIRE III

1. He refuses to have Daenerys Targaryen assassinated

2. Lord Varys

3. It has three eyes

4. Lily Allen.

5. Sandor "the Hound" Clegane

6. Tywin Lannister

7. The High Septon

8. As a punishment for conducting unethical experiments on living subjects

9. He is executed by Robb Stark

10. A pirate ship

A HUNT FOR WORDS III

M	A	E	R	I	E	S	M	A	R	W	Y	L	L	A
A	Y	J	D	L	T	E	K	E	L	R	U	K	A	A
C	C	L	D	J	V	A	R	D	I	S	N	R	N	D
O	Y	J	E	G	D	U	M	E	F	K	K	Y	O	O
R	X	Y	D	S	T	E	P	C	N	U	A	W	D	O
N	N	Z	N	L	R	E	B	M	O	L	I	O	H	W
E	D	M	U	N	D	N	L	A	N	L	Y	L	A	N
E	S	V	O	B	O	M	M	U	L	P	P	L	D	O
T	Y	Z	S	D	N	N	S	F	C	L	D	I	N	R
A	L	N	A	R	R	K	O	U	L	A	E	W	A	Y
E	L	L	O	C	K	E	L	T	O	S	Y	R	D
R	E	H	T	A	E	W	Y	R	R	E	M	E	R	B
G	M	S	L	T	O	R	G	O	N	A	L	Y	U	D
N	E	B	B	I	K	N	Y	W	E	L	M	C	R	P
N	A	M	O	W	G	N	I	P	E	E	W	F	W	K

DAARIO AND THE GREY WORM

The Grey Worm is correct. Although there are more possible routes to success from 18 tosses, these extra success routes are not quite sufficient to overcome the basic problem, which is that rolling three sixes from 18 is broadly similar to rolling one 6 from six tosses 3 times in a row. The actual chances of making the roll, if you are curious, are 0.66 for the six-toss roll, and 0.60 for the 18-toss roll.

KHALEESI OF THORNS

4.5 miles. The difference between the speeds means the time is split 3:1 between slower and faster. 6hrs x ¾ = 4.5hrs at 1mph (and 1.5hrs at 3mph)

QARTH

$\frac{1}{7}$ is approximately 0.14285, so 19 is around 114.28 percent of the answer. $19 \div 114.285 \times 100$ gives a stack size of 16.625, but that knowledge didn't help Xaro any.

TWO TWINS

A pair of scales.

BRIDGER CERWYN

Consider $x = 3y$, and $x + 18 = 2y + 36$. Therefore $x = 2y + 36\text{-}18$, or $2y + 18$. As $x = 3y$, we know $3y = 2y + 18$, or $y = 18$. Then, x has to be 54. Eighteen years ago, Bridger was 54 and Beedie 18; now they are 72 and 36.

MEN WITHOUT HATS

There was. If Barth has hair, he is being observed by
Mudge; if he is bald, he is looking at Gergen.

THE GREAT OTHER

The maximum is 24, 3 + 5 + 7 + 9. The minimum is
16, 7 + 9, for the nine who see through one
eye can also double up as the three blind in
one eye and, because it doesn't say otherwise, the
five who see normally.

VALAR MORGHULIS

We are told that the door and window were locked and sealed and that there was no other way in or out. With sorcery off the table, that means the murderer still has to be inside. Since there's nowhere to hide, the murderer must be in plain sight. Ser Normon had to have killed himself and staged the argument to make his family think he'd been murdered.

PLAYING THE FIELD

To meet the conditions, the field will need to be 501,760 acres in size, with the fence having the same number of bars, and would be some 28 miles long on each side.

ALLYCE & WILLIT

Willitt and Rolf were back-to-back.

THE PLANK

Some of the wood is lost as sawdust, so each piece
now weighs less than 2.5lb.

LAZY LEO

The error is in thinking that the two situations, gain
or lose, are directly comparable. They're entirely separate.
The loss goes from two silver stags to one stag, and the
gain goes from one stag to two stags, so the magnitudes are
the same, and it's a flat $^{50}/_{50}$ as to whether you gain or lose.

A QUIZ OF
ICE AND FIRE IV

1. The King in the North

2. Robert Baratheon's will

3. Winterfell

4. Petyr "Littlefinger" Baelish

5. King-Beyond-the-Wall

6. Stannis Baratheon

7. The Free City of Myr

8. Her largest dragon

9. The Blackfish

10. Jaime Lannister

A HUNDRED GEMS

Taking the most expensive first, 19 camels will cost 95 opals. One ass will bring that to 20 animals for 96 opals. Finally, the remaining four opals buy 80 goats, taking us to 100 opals exchanged for 100 animals.

PEARLS OF WISDOM

The second bag has a better chance, two-thirds, of holding a pearl. The first bag has just a flat one-half chance.

GOLD AND GREEN

You need a pair of square numbers that total 100, and the square root of one has to be three-quarters of the square root of the other. There's only nine square numbers less than 100, with square roots 1–9. A moment's thought will reveal that the two which add to 100 are 36 and 64, and their square roots are six and eight, which fit.

AS THE RAVEN FLIES

Draw a perpendicular line from Cider Hall to the direct Longtable-Ashford road, and call the spot where it hits that road 'X'. You then have two right-angled triangles, (a) Longtable-X-Cider Hall, and (b) Ashford-X-Cider Hall. Both A and B share a side of length 12, from Cider Hall to X. From Pythagoras's theorem, there are only two right-angled triangles that have one side of length 12 – so because Cider Hall is nearer Longtable than Ashford, (a) is 12, 9, 15 and (b) is 12, 16, 20. We know the indirect distance is 35, so that has to be the 15-length hypotenuse from (a) and the 20-length hypotenuse from (b). The two sides of length 12 are the distance between Cider Hall and the road. That means that the two sides forming the straight road Longtable-X and X-Ashford have to be the remaining 9 and 16. So it's 25 miles from Longtable to Ashford direct

THE DAWN'S DELAY

Time.

REDFORT

Mychel will be half his father's age in $70 \div 3 = 23$ years and four months, so $x + 23.33 = (y + 23.33) \div 2$, or $2x + 23.33 = y$. Additionally, from Lord Horton's first statement, $6x = y$. So $2x + 23.33 = 6x$, or $x = 23.33 \div 4$, and Mychel is five years and ten months old. That makes Lord Horton 35, and, subtracting knowns from 70, Lady Houtella 29 years and two months old.

RAYDER'S TOWER

The series of moves to escape the tower is as follows: 1. Put bundle in at top. It drops to bottom. 2. Put Ynga in at top. She drops, raising the bundle. 3. Switch the bundle for Stig. He drops, raising Ynga. 4. Ynga gets out at top, Stig gets out at bottom. Put bundle in, dropping it to bottom. 5. Stig gets in with bundle at bottom. Val gets in at top, raising Stig and bundle. Stig gets out at top, Val gets out at bottom. 6. Repeat steps 1–4, except that the bundle starts already in the basket. Now Ynga is at the top. 7. Ynga gets in at top, raising bundle. She gets out at the bottom, joining the other two. The bundle, now unopposed, drops to the bottom as well.

FAIR ISLE

Considering the requirements as simultaneous equations, you need to ensure that the nine terms spread across the five variable types sum to 18. You will find that there are eight possible ways to add nine multiples of 1, 2, 3, 4 and 0 to 18. From these eight options, there are three different ways to pick five unique sets. Labelling the casks from A = 4 gal to E = 0 gal, one brother has to have $3A + B + C + D + 3E$ casks. The other four brothers can have any two of the following three pairs:

$$(A + 3B + 2C + D + 2E \text{ and } 2A + B + 2C + 3D + E),$$

$$(A + 3B + C + 3D + E \text{ and } 2A + B + 3C + D + 2E),$$

and $(A + 2B + 3C + 2D + E \text{ and } 2A + 2B + C + 2D + 2E)$

LADIES, NOT IN WAITING

Twice as many again means three times the current total. For x and 3x to fall equal distances either side of ten, they have to be five and 15. So there are five ladies.

SER ONDRE

Enrike cheated. There's no way you could go that distance through the desert under the noon sun with a single flask of water and still have water left to sweat out, no matter how well conditioned you were. He either found a lot of water en route, or cut a big chunk of the distance out.

A HUNT FOR WORDS IV

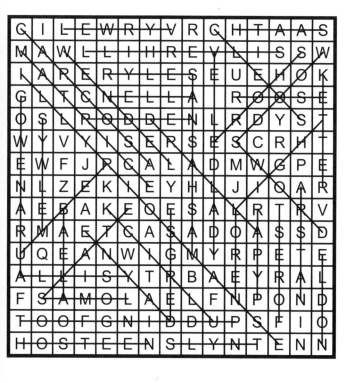

G	I	L	E	W	R	Y	V	R	G	H	T	A	A	S
M	A	W	L	L	I	H	R	E	V	L	I	S	S	W
I	A	R	E	R	Y	L	E	S	E	U	E	H	O	K
G	L	T	C	N	E	L	L	A		R	O	O	S	E
O	S	L	R	O	D	D	E	N	L	R	D	Y	S	T
W	Y	V	Y	I	S	E	R	S	E	S	C	R	H	T
E	W	F	J	R	C	A	L	A	D	M	W	G	P	E
N	L	Z	E	K	I	E	Y	H	L	J	I	O	A	R
A	E	B	A	K	E	O	E	S	A	L	R	T	R	V
R	M	A	E	T	C	A	S	A	D	O	A	S	S	D
U	Q	E	A	N	W	I	G	M	Y	R	P	E	T	E
A	L	L	I	S	Y	T	R	B	A	E	Y	R	A	L
F	S	A	M	O	L	A	E	L	F	N	P	O	N	D
T	O	O	F	G	N	I	D	D	U	P	S	F	I	O
H	O	S	T	E	E	N	S	L	Y	N	T	E	N	N

A FOOL'S GAME

To calculate a summed there-and-back distance for each node in the path, multiply out the number of nodes, x, by $(x-1)$ – trips – and $(2x-1)$ – odd number distances. Then divide by 3, for terms. $50 \times 49 \times 99 \div 3$ gives you a total distance of 80,850 yards, which is well over 45 miles.

BREA'S FEAST

One man can fill all four roles, given the right set of familial intermarriages.

GOODBROOK

The stable master lends a horse of his own to the herd, to bring the total to 18. Then the eldest son gets $18 \div 2 = 9$ horses, the middle son gets $18 \div 3 = 6$, and the youngest son gets $18 \div 9 = 2$. Since $9 + 6 + 2 = 17$, that leaves the stable master's loan horse, which he reclaims.

SIMEON STAR-EYES

Hang the hat on the arrow before firing. You may not hit the target, but you'll certainly shoot through the hat.

THE DOOR'S GUARD

A key.

BAQQ

There are three possible combinations of winning with just one dice $(\frac{1}{6} \times \frac{5}{6} \times \frac{5}{6}) \times 3 - \frac{75}{216}$. There are three possible combinations of winning with two dice $(\frac{1}{6} \times \frac{1}{6} \times \frac{5}{6}) \times 3 - \frac{15}{216}$, but these are worth double $- \frac{30}{216}$. There is obviously only one way of winning with all three dice $- \frac{1}{216}$ and this is worth triple $- \frac{3}{216}$. Combining these odds $(75 + 30 + 3) \div 216 - \frac{108}{216}$, or 0.5 – an even chance.

ALSO AVAILABLE

Sherlock Holmes' Elementary Puzzles

978-1-78097-578-8

Alice's Puzzles in Wonderland

978-1-78097-675-4

The Medieval Puzzle Collection

978-1-78097-577-1